Calm Your Storms and Move Your Mountains

MARTINA IGWE

Copyright © 2025 AEGA Design Publishing

All rights reserved. No part of this publication may be reproduced, distributed, or transmitted in any form or by any means, including photocopying, recording, or other electronic or mechanical methods, without the prior written permission of the publisher, except in the case of brief quotations embodied in critical reviews and certain other noncommercial uses permitted by copyright law.

ISBN (e-book) 978-1-0685398-6-2
ISBN (hardcover) 978-1-0685398-4-8

AEGA Design Publishing Ltd Kemp House
160 City Road, London, EC1V 2NX
United Kingdom
info@aegadesign.co.uk
www.aegadesign.co.uk

Printed in the United Kingdom

CONTENTS

Acknowledgments v
Introduction vii

Chapter 1: The Waves and the Storms of Life 1
Chapter 2: The Promise of Abundant Life 9
Chapter 3: Why You Need the Word of God 13
Chapter 4: Fill Your Mind with the Word 21
Chapter 5: Speak Out What You Believe 27
Chapter 6: Speak Life Not Death 34
Chapter 7: Let the Holy Spirit Teach You 38

Conclusion 46
References 48
Autobiography 50
About the Author. 51

ACKNOWLEDGMENTS

I give glory to the Almighty God who had given me the grace to write this book. Many thanks to my family for their moral support. My sincere appreciation goes to Mr. Gerald Ward, librarian, and Sacramento Public Library's I Street Press for the effort they put into helping new writers like me.

INTRODUCTION

This is a book written to help readers to understand that they could still stay strong in their tough times or when they are undergoing some adversities of life. Weariness of the soul, worries, anxieties discouragements, or even depression can set in within the heart of anybody if faced with overwhelming situations. There is the belief that one can receive strength in the inner man to pass through such times and even to overcome by building up one's faith through the Word of God. We were told in the Scriptures that David the king encouraged himself in the Lord.

CHAPTER 1

The Waves and the Storms of life

So often we hear people talk about the hurricanes, the whirlwinds, the cyclones etc. of moving body of waters, and in fact, we have people who are called storm watchers, whose job it is to monitor storms and waves to categorize them and even give them names and also warn people about them.

They rise and move with great force with moving water. Some are called tropical storms. They can be so powerful that they can destroy things on their way. They can overturn boats or ships so sometimes people are advised to evacuate from the route of the storms and move to safe areas. They produce tides and turbulence.

The waves are associated with the oceans, seas, or rivers and so on. Bottom line is that when they rise up, they may create problems as they move for whatsoever maybe on their route. Storms create a sense of fear and uncertainty

Jesus traveled a lot on the boat with his disciples, and they were well-aware of the sea waves. Once the waves arose while He was asleep in the boat and the boat was getting filled with water, there was a sense of danger, so his disciples cried out to him (Mk 4:38).

We hear people talk about when the tsunami hits and also the cyclones.

The storms and waves and the high winds can produce so much noise that they are said to roar. The thought that comes to the mind is that of fear and destruction and imminent danger. Hence there is a desire to avoid and protect oneself from them. When people on boat ride encounters storms waves or high winds, they throw out some of their loads or belongings into the river or sea in order to reduce the weight of the boat to prevent it from capsizing or overturning into the sea. In such a case, there will be a lot of apprehension tension and confusion. Many life struggles present themselves in this manner.

Torrential rainfall can be so much that they generate so much run off water that is called flood. The floods can be so much that they constitute flood disasters, causing a lot of troubles and damages and people can get drowned in them or lose their properties. So you talk about enemies rising up like a flood or talk about the rising waters or roaring flood because of the sense of uncertainty and pain that they carry with them we want to make all efforts to overcome those struggles as soon as possible.

So we can ask God to help us avert some of these turbulences of life by speaking the promises of God regarding the issues that are troubling us. We can ask God to cancel impending ones proclaiming our victory as its written in the word. God can also turn the tide of the oceans or rolling waters to our favor if we continue to declare his promises.

When Jesus was woken up in the boat because of the looming waves and water that was threatening him and his disciples, he got up and spoke to the wind. He said, "Peace, be still," and immediately, there was great calm.

In another example as Peter tried to walk on the water with Jesus, the roaring and raging waves from the water frightened Peter, and he became afraid of the waters. He began to sink, and he had to cry out to the master. He did not keep quiet. He said, "Lord, save me," and Jesus grabbed him and kept him from drowning.

The Mountains of Life

When we talk about mountains, what comes to the mind is an elevated physical structure that sometimes rises above the ground level, maybe higher than the hills mostly made of rocks. Mountains block your views so you cannot see the other side. They are not objects that can be easily swept away by regular brooms or brushes. Those that know much about mountains know that they are mostly removed or broken down by strong blasts for those who work in the concrete industry or there about. In life people use the word mountain to describe life obstacles or limitations. Mountains on your path of journey can mean a delayed journey or disrupted journey. A mountain on your way may mean that you would spend a longer time trying to achieve your goal in a particular area of life.

On the spiritual perspective, mountains of life can present itself also as problem or lacks and struggles arising in an individual's life, physically, mentally, socially, financially, marriage, children, and so on. When the person is burdened so much, it could lead to things like depression and anxiety. Some are referred to as mountains of sickness,

mountains of family issues, mountains of delay, mountains of stagnation, and so on. Satan plants these things in the life of a Christian to make that person discouraged and miserable. People talk about mountains of troubles confronting them.

Jesus used the word mountain as he was talking to his disciples when he said if they had faith as little as a mustard seed that they are able to command the mountains to be moved and it will obey them (Mt 17:20). He encouraged them to speak to the mountain before them so the mountains could move. Situations of life that seems difficult are looked upon as insurmountable mountains.

In the wilderness the children of Israel encountered a lot of obstacles which we can also describe as mountains and those constituted a lot of struggles for them. Examples included their experience with the walls of Jericho.

People say don't tell God how big your mountains are, but tell your mountains how big your God is. So what happens is that we want the mountains on our way to be made plain or leveled. We want them to be moved or for them to become valleys. Sometimes, God can give the grace to climb the mountain.

We are made to understand that the grace of God, accompanied by his might, can help us confront our life struggles, as we pray and also use the sword of the Word of God in our tongue to speak to our situations and circumstances;

> Then he answered and he spoke unto me saying, "This is the word of the Lord unto Zerubabel, saying not by might nor by power but by my spirit," says the lord of Hosts. Who art thou o great mountain before Zerubabel thou shall become a plain. (Zec 4:4–7)

We know fully well that the storms and the mountains along our paths are ill-winds that does nobody any good. There is the need for us to agree with what God says about us. Obstacles and limitations distract our full attention to God as we are busy trying to remove them for a full length of time. There is the need for us to partner with God and resist them for example sickness or disease the devil might deceive you and use it to destroy your body. When we are attacked by evil situations and we allow God to intervene concerning it, he is able to turn things around for our good.

If you do not resist the devil and his properties, he has no other agenda but to destroy. So be careful when you say God is sending evil to you to teach you some lessons because he says, "For I know the thoughts that I think towards you say the lord the thought of peace and not of evil to give you an expected end" (Jer 29:11).

So as our faith is built up in the Word of God, we begin to speak forth what we believe as we speak his word, and his promises are activated in our lives.

Jesus came to offer us eternal life. A life filled with God's, love, goodness, mercies, and grace in great measures. The believer is encouraged to believe God for forgiveness, joy, peace, good health, long life, and every good thing that the blood of Jesus has made available for God's people as we have in this scripture, "Beloved I wish in all things that thou mayest prosper and be in good health as your soul prospers" (3 Jn 1:2).

Whenever the enemy comes with his attacks, we resist them by God's word.

CHAPTER 2

The Promise of Abundant Life

Jesus Christ referred to himself as the good shepherd who would pastor his sheep and bring them to safety and feed them with good pasture unlike the enemy who would only come to do them harm. "The thief cometh not but for to steal to kill and to destroy. But I am come that you may have life and life more abundantly" (Jn 10:10).

Despite the presence of challenges and obstacles that life may throw at us God's will for his people is for them to prosper. Satan rejoices when God's people suffer, but God does not do that. It is an opportunity for the enemy to clap his hands, but if we allow God into our situation, he is able to turn it around and take all the glory. The grace of God is available for whosoever will believe. Jesus did not come to arrest and judge humanity. He came to make peace. He went about doing good throughout his lifetime. He healed the sick, raised the dead, covered people's shame, etc. He preached the Word of God when he had the chance, and whenever people needed instant miracles, he did just that. A hungry man can't hear you until you give him food.

The will of God for man is for man to flourish in all the things that concerns him. He created Adam and Eve and put them in a beautiful garden—a garden that was filled with everything they could ever need. When man lost the dominion that God gave them, God still sent his son, Jesus Christ, to redeem and restore it to mankind through the cross of Calvary. Take a look. "Dear friend, I pray that you may enjoy good health and that all may go well with you even as your soul is getting along well."

God's wish for humanity is a good wish therefore many of the obstacles we come across in life cannot be mostly traced to him. He loved humanity that his son shed his blood for our sins even before many of us were born. Like it is said in the following scripture, "For God so loved the world that he gave his only begotten son that whosoever believeth in him should not perish but have everlasting life" (Jn 3:16).

An asthmatic patient that is gasping for breath cannot hear any single word that you are saying until you minister healing to him, then he can breathe, calm down, and listen to your message.

Sometimes, we may find ourselves in the midst of some situations or circumstances in life that may be overwhelming that the only thing that can give us peace of mind is in reminding ourselves about what the Word of God said, "You will keep him in perfect peace, whose mind is stayed on You" (Is 26:3).

We know that God's will for his children is abundant life, so in an effort to establish that promise in our lives, we want to cooperate with God and his words to bring it to fulfilment. As soon as our inner eyes are opened to know this truth, we begin to find out more of God's provisions for us through Jesus Christ his son and we ask God to make it a reality in our lives. There is a whole lot of promises of God pertaining to various areas of life, waiting for the believer to locate them and appropriate them in their situations and circumstances.

Apart from fasting or praying, worshiping or thanksgiving, and so on, every Christian is encouraged to develop an interest in the Word of God. A word from God might change our situations. Many people in the Bible that walked closely with God had a word from God that they were holding unto until God's purpose came to pass in their lives.

Examples include Abraham, Moses, Joshua, Mary, etc.

You either agree with God and what he says about your life or you agree with Satan and the enemy and their plans for your life. Stop going to church for church's sake.

Familiarize yourself with God's word it is for your benefits.

CHAPTER 3

Why You Need the Word of God

We are told in the scriptures that the Gospel is the power of God by which he saves us. God uses the foolishness of preaching his Word to save and deliver and heal people. So the importance of the Word of God cannot be over emphasized. "For I am not ashamed of the Gospel of Christ for it is the power of God unto salvation to everyone that believeth" (Rom 1:16).

So we see that we need God's words more than ever. It is the building block with which God builds our lives.

When we study God's words, we get filled with his

Word, we get to know him more. We know the things that he likes and the things that he does not like. So his Words are very important more, so that it was his Spirit that motivated those people that wrote the Bible.

"All scripture is given by inspiration of God and is profitable for doctrine for reprove for correction for instruction in righteousness that the man of God might be complete thoroughly equipped for every good work" (2 Tm 3:16–17 NKJV)

We need God's word because he tells us to bind it to our heart for our own benefit.

"This book of the law shall not depart out of thy mouth but thou shall meditate there in day and night that thou mayest make thy way prosperous" (Jo 1:8).

God is encouraging us to learn and rehearse the Word of God because we will be blessed as we do so. As we search the Word of God, we learn about him and his goodness and the promises that he provided for us in his Word. When you are facing challenges, you can only come against them by the Word of God that is in your heart.

We search and study the Word of God for guidance. It illuminates our way. It helps us make right decisions. "Your word is a lamp unto my feet and a light to my path" (Ps 119:105).

When we study the Word of God, we are doing the right thing as a believer that is the only way to find out the truth about God and his words, that way, we can be firmly rooted in his word. "Study to show yourself approved unto God a workman that needeth not to be ashamed rightly dividing the word of truth." (2 Tm 2:15 KJV).

When you are trying to claim God's promises in a particular area of your life, there may be hinderances, mountains, and storms limiting you, and you will need to stand on the Word of God to overcome them. The mountains will need to be moved or leveled, and the storms need to be stopped. You need peace.

God created order out of a disorderly situation by speaking words. Genesis 1:1–3a says,

> In the beginning God cre-
> ated the heavens and the

earth. Now the earth was formless and empty, darkness was over the surface of the deep and the spirit of the lord was hovering over the waters. And God said let there be light and there was light.

So we are permitted to address any form of destructions that come our way and speak what the Word of God says over them, so we can overcome them. If you allow challenges to stay, they may choke life out of you. So everybody is encouraged to rise up to the task.

When Jesus was speaking to Peter because Peter recognized him as the Christ, he made Peter some promises including this, "I will give you the keys of the kingdom of heaven whatever you bind on earth shall be bound in heaven and whatever you lose in the earth shall be loosed in heaven" (Mt 16:20 NIV). Here we can allow or disallow certain things from taking place in our lives by standing on this Word of God. God will honor his word.

Your faith in God will be strengthened as you feed your mind with the Word of God. Sometimes you need to take responsibility and pray for yourself, declaring the Word of God over yourself and your situation because in some cases, people's prayers may not work for you until you actually get the spiritual understanding of what is going on. Stand on the Word of God and take authority over the situation by yourself. You need to study or have a knowledge of the Word of God, so your faith can grow. As you do that, the word multiplies and your faith is built up then you are able to apply God's word for results. Your faith can move mountains. Your faith can cause you to speak the Word of God to still your storms.

So faith is actually your response to God's word. We need to speak our deliverance by what God already declared in his Word. When we say what God says, it becomes a sword and performs what God says. "So is my word that goes out from my mouth. It will not return to me empty but will accomplish what I desire and achieve the purpose for which I sent it" (Is 55:11).

God says none of his words shall fall to the ground, and that means we can depend on his word to come to pass in our lives. The Word of God is the sword of the spirit. As we release it against satanic attacks, our victory awaits us.

We search the Word of God because he says to remind him of what his word says. So when we speak his Word, we are giving his Words back to him. We learn God's words so we can remind him of his promises to us. "Put me in remembrance. Let us argue together set forth your case that you may be proved right" (Is 43:26 NIV).

God spoke the world into existence, so let us feel free to speak our desires according to his will to pass for our lives also. Command the yokes of darkness and the enemy to break off from your life. Address them with the Word of God. They can hear when you speak by faith to them, and they will adhere to the Word of God that you speak to them.

Jesus performed miracles through various means. Sometimes by touching, sometimes by prayer and thanksgiving, sometimes by giving commands, and majority of the time, by speaking the Word. He told the man from Capernaum to go home because his son was well already. "'Go.' Jesus replied, "'Your son will live.' The man took Jesus at his word and departed." (Jn 4:50 NIV).

Before the centurion got home, the son was healed already. Just like the Scripture said, "He sent his word and healed them and delivered them from their destruction" (Ps 107:20).

Facing Your Limitations

The Scripture encourages us to face the mountains and tell them what we want them to do by faith. Do we want them to grow bigger? The answer is no. We want them to become plain. We want them to become valleys with gardens that are well-planted with good trees, flowers, and so on and so forth. We are not alone in the battle against the mountains God himself helps with the fight. "Who art thou o great mountain before Zerubbabel thou shall become a plain and shall bring forth the headstone thereof" (Zec 4:7 KJV).

We are reminded in verse 6, it is not by our power nor by our might that these mighty things shall be done but by the spirit of the living God. Amen.

Satan tempted our Lord, Jesus Christ, three different times when he was fasting. He replied him with the words of God each time. But he answered and said it is written that man shall not live by bread alone but by every word that comes out of the mouth of God (Mt 4:4).

So we see that Jesus spoke the word to defend himself from Satan. At the end of the day Satan went away. The same thing would happen when we speak the Word of God to any challenges.

CHAPTER 4

Fill Your Mind with the Word

Battles are fought first in the mind and then lost or won in the mind before the manifestation in the physical. When you store up enough of God's words in your heart, you are able to speak it.

"Let the Word of God dwell in you richly in all wisdom teaching and admonishing one another in psalms and hymns and spiritual songs singing with grace in your hearts to the Lord" (Col 3:16 KJV). When you feed on God's words, it fills you with divine wisdom. You will find out that the Bible has information about almost every aspect of life. The Bible sometimes looks hard to read, more so to study. But if you are just beginning, why not just start with getting to know some interesting life stories in the Bible first that will kindle your interest more.

You can check out stories about Joseph and his coat of many colors. Read about Abraham and Sarah and their miracle child Isaac. There is the story about David and Goliath. Talk of Samson. Talk about Esther. Talk of the wall of Jericho. What shall we say about Christ Jesus and the New Testament. There is a whole lot to find out if you can find time for the Word of God, but you have to develop interest by beginning from somewhere.

The more you know, the more you can practice and live your life by the Word of God and let it bear fruit in you as you speak. "Out of the abundance of the mind the mouth speaks" (Lk 6:45).

God ministers words of encouragement to your heart. At the same time, also Satan, the enemy of your soul, is ministering fear and discouragements to your mind. That is why you have to guard your heart. Fill your heart with God's word, so you can have enough knowledge to draw from, to fight your struggles. In situations like this, it's like there is a fight in your spirit to break you free from the roaring of the enemy, speaking negativity in your heart. It is called a good fight of faith. "Fight the good fight of faith, lay hold of eternal life, whereunto thou art also called, and has professed a good profession before many witnesses" (1 Tm 6:12).

Let us plant the Word of God in our heart. As we read and ingest it into our mind, we have a store laid up, and we can draw from these to face challenges or circumstance as the need arises in our daily lives. As we hide the word of God in our hearts, we are able to ponder on it, to rehearse them, and to speak them to our situations. If you do not fill your mind with the Word of God, your heart would be burdened by fears cares and worries.

One of the ways not to dwell on the fear and negative thoughts that are flooding your mind from the enemy is to have a Word ready in your heart for every situation, reminding yourself of the goodness of God and his promises in the Word of God that has been promised to you in the Scriptures. Read the Bible and find out what the Word of God says about you. Look for the people that understand the Word of God more than you do and learn from their teachings. Ask the Holy Spirit to teach you the Word of God as you pray.

I prefer to repeat the Word of God over my life than to repeat the negative prophecies of others over my life. As we do that, we are reminding God about his promise over us.

It's better to ponder over the love of God and the goodness of God, to review the mercies of God and his testimonies than to be heavy laden with worries and anxieties, and to put our trust and hope in Christ and his Word.

Think about the promises of God concerning your health, finances, mental, spiritual life, His promises about your family life, social life, peace of mind, and joy. As you think on these, you will worry less. Your faith is built up, and you speak out what you believe. "For all the promises of God in him are yea and in him. Amen unto the glory of God by us" (2 Cor 1:20).

Refuse to meditate on your negative circumstances. Instead, put them before God in prayer. Then search out Scriptures that speak about your ordained victories in these areas and wrap your mind around them. As you do so, your mindset is renewed. You receive strength from your inside for your daily life.

> Finally, brethren whatsoever is true whatever is noble whatever is just whatever is pure whatever is lovely whatever things are of good report if there is any virtue and if there is anything praiseworthy meditate on these things. (Phil 4:8 NKJV)

As you refuse to think negative thoughts but choose to be filled with good and positive thoughts from the Word of God, the enemy of your soul, Satan, is unable to have a hold on your mind, and God fights your battle.

As your mind is renewed by God's Word, you notice that it affects the way you speak. You are encouraged to speak more positively on yourself than speaking the language of the enemy, which is filled with frustrations and unbelief.

Your mind is filled with the promises of God for your life as you meditate once a while. When you are confronted with difficult situations, you are able to draw strength from the Word in your heart, and you begin to speak them forth on your situations as your faith is built up and you make declarations. Yokes will be broken.

CHAPTER 5

Speak Out What You Believe

The preachers of the Word of God do so mainly because of their confidence in the Word of God. They know that the Word of God works. If you can believe them by faith practice or speak them to yourself, situations and circumstances would turn around for your good. Going to church without learning the Word of God by yourself is like going to school without a pen. You cannot confess the word of God until you learn it, and you are able to remember them. You find out that when you repeat the Word of God to yourself your faith in the word of God rises up and you are able to make bold declaration regarding your expectations over your limitations. Declaring what you believe.

"Let the redeemed of the Lord say so" (Ps 107:2 NIV). When we speak God's Word over situations, the angel of the Lord can hear us speaking, and they help carry out what the command in that Word of God says. "Bless the Lord ye his angels, who excel in strength, who do his word, heeding the voice of his word" (Ps 103:20 KJV)

The enemy will not give way in some situation until they see your confidence in the Word of God as you declare it by faith. In spite of the limitations, we go back to the promises of God and encourage ourselves in them and speak over them by faith.

When you go to bed at night, think on the Word of God. As you meditate on his Word, your life is changed to conform to what his words says. "As a man thinks in his heart so is he" (Prv 23:7a).

Challenge your circumstances with the Word of God. Repeat what the Word of God says about your situation. When you pray, remind God about his promises.

Ask him to bring his Word to pass in your life

The Word of God is the sword of the Spirit. It is the sword with which you fight your spiritual battles. It is the rod of God, coming from your mouth to confront your opposition.

David spoke to Goliath first, declaring his belief and trust in the God of Israel before throwing his sling at Goliath. So while Goliath was making his declarations at David, he came, trusting in his physical strength and sword while David depended on God's power with just a sling and small stones, having declared his victory from the beginning

Learn to shut down negative voices speaking to your heart. Repeat God's word to them, and they will leave you alone. Read out the Word of God to yourself every day, whenever you can. Challenge the spirit of fear that is overwhelming your heart with the Word of God. Resist the voice in your mind that is telling you that you are about to lose your mental stability. Say to yourself, "God has not given me the spirit of fear but of love of power and of sound mind" (2 Tm 1:7).

Speak to that feeling that is saying you are going to die you can say, "I shall not die. I shall live to declare the works of God" (Ps 118:17).

Pertaining to your health, you can read so many healing Scriptures to yourself every day and stand on your belief in them. Keep taking your medications. If you are already on them, keep speaking the Word until you are totally healed. Example include, "For they are life to those that find them and health to all their flesh" (Prv 4:22).

As we make our faith declarations over our lives, let's not forget to declare God's goodness and favor in our lives on a daily basis for by strength shall no man prevail we depend on his grace. "For you, Lord, bless the righteous you surround him with favor as a shield" (Ps 5:12 NIV).

When you are in doubt of the goodness of God remember also Scriptures like, "Blessed be the lord who daily loadeth us with his benefits even the God of our salvation" (Ps 68:19).

Remember also this scripture when talking about

your needs, "The lord is my shepherd I shall not want" (Ps 23:1).

God wants us to have more than surplus in all areas of our life. On the other hand, Satan wants us to be filled with lack, and he wants the joy of God's children to be minimized by all means. The enemy of your soul, the devil, is happy each time you speak his language instead of speaking the promises of God.

Each time you speak negativity, you are cooperating with the enemy to bring his wishes to pass in your life. But whenever you repeat God's Words and promises over your life, you cooperate with God by speaking life and not destruction, "From the fruit of their lips people are filled with good things" (Prv 12:14a).

You can use statements like "God is able," "The Lord is my strength," and many other examples from the Bible to encourage yourself. Refuse to use certain phrases when you speak instead of saying, "I am dying to drink a cup of coffee," why don't you say, "I can't wait to drink a cup of coffee." That sounds better. Minimize or stop, if you can, the use of words like, "Over your dead body." Why don't we develop phrases like, "I love you to life," and not "I love you to death?"

Seek out the promises of God from the Scriptures. Internalize them. Meditate on them and repeat them to yourself whenever you can. As you repeat them to your hearing, you are releasing those words and the anointing of God behind them into your life and future. The word of God empowers you for certain things as you acquaint yourself with them. It gives you the faith to rise up and decree and declare to bring God's expectations for our lives to pass.

There are certain battles in your life that you can easily overcome if you knew the exact Scriptures to speak and stand on those Scriptures by faith. I wish that every believer would be taught this message as early as possible in their Christian faith. This help them avoid, overcome, or navigate through some life struggles. "And they overcame him by the blood of the lamb. and by the word of their testimony" (Rv 12:11a).

When you speak the promises of God, they go before you into unforeseen situations so that when the time comes, the Word is waiting to intervene in your situation. It is a mystery and may be hard for some of us who did not really have Christian teachers to learn from when we were young in the faith.

Learn to speak your words of faith over your situations. Use your words against the adversary Satan. You have the authority so use your words. "Where the word of a king is, there is power." (Eccl 8:4).

CHAPTER 6

Speak Life Not Death

Speak faith filled words and not doubt.

Do not speak your fear or anxiety. As you allow the Word of God to dwell richly in your heart, and you meditate on them so very often, your mind is renewed, your faith is built stronger, and you begin to be more positive on your view of life than being negative. You begin to see yourself the way God sees you and how the Word of God describes you, and this will help you to begin to say and declare the victories that Christ had bought for you with his blood. You also begin to claim the promises of God for yourself. You refuse to speak fear because that is what your enemy the devil wants you to do.

Do not confess the fear that is in your heart but say that which the Word of God declares over that situation. This means that even though you are aware of the crisis in that particular area, you believe that God will cause you to overcome in that situation according to his Word.

Though you may be weak in your body, the Scripture encourages us to declare our healing according to God's promises even as we believe God or seek for medical help. It encourages us to declare our victories in Christ in the face of adversity. "Let the weak say I am strong" (Jl 3:10).

Do not keep talking about your problem all the time. Speak the promises of God too. Say to yourself, "Even though I am struggling in this area, my hope lies in what the Word of God says about it."

When Caleb and Joshua, along with others, were asked to describe what the land they viewed looked like, the majority gave negative declarations, while the two of them spoke favorably regarding the journey and both of them got good rewards. Encourage your heart in the Word of God, and speak it forth it would yield its fruits. As you do that, you are speaking life unto your dead situations, and you are calling them back to life as you address them. "Death and life is in the power of the tongue and those who love it eat the fruit thereof" (Prv 18:21).

So let us learn to only say what God said about our situations and circumstances so that we can get the result he wants us to get. Your words are powerful. When you speak faith-filled words, you use them to create or build the things you expect for your future according to his promises.

We need God to help us in this area. When we pray for our breakthroughs or miracles, let us continue to speak according to our faith as the days go by. Let us not cancel that, which we have prayed and believed, by speaking unfavorably about it again. Use the rod of God in your mouth and speak rightly as you have believed

By faith the people of Israel defeated the people of Jericho by singing and chanting just like God commanded them as we read in the book of Joshua. It was literally a mountain planted by the enemy to block their passage. But the grace of God was made available to them. They did not have to fight with their arrows and bows. As the Lord commanded Joshua, they marched around the city for some days, blew the trumpets, and gave a loud shout out and the walls fell apart and crumbled. "When the trumpet sounded the army shouted and at the sound of the trumpet, when the men gave a loud shout, the wall collapsed" (Jo 6:20).

This is an illustration that God can also fight our battles for us by his grace or favor, not necessarily by physical force. The gates of Jericho were shut against the Israelites but shouts of victory broke them open because the Lord was with his people. Today as we speak the Word over our lives and situations, as we stand on it by faith believing God to bring his promises to pass in our lives, we are practicing the Word of God, and it will yield unto us that which we desire from the Lord.

Sometimes, you need to stand on your feet pick up the promises of God and run with them. This is what the ministers of God also do in their closets. They internalize the Word of God, and they use it to fight against the enemy or life struggles.

CHAPTER 7

Let the Holy Spirit Teach You

As we fill our hearts with God's word, starting gradually in our own capacity, starting simply with parts of the Bible that we can easily understand or enjoy reading—i.e., reading or listening to the written Word of God called logos— let us remember to ask the spirit of God to read along with us so that he can teach us the Word as we read. The holy spirit of God makes the word of God to come alive in us as we study his Word, and he also helps us to interpret the word of God as we study.

As we come across issues of life, and we need some

help, the spirit of God will lead us to the particular scripture that will encourage us or lift us out of our situations. This is the reason why we need to familiarize ourselves with the word of God. As we involve the Holy Spirit, he gives us or refers to us the word that will lift us out of our situation. This particular word is meant for us to personalize and use to our advantage, reminding God of what he had promised us.

Faith in the Word of God may not just spring up in our hearts instantly but begin from somewhere. Start slowly and steadily repeat to yourself whenever you have the chance, and gradually, your mind and spirit will internalize it until you begin to quote it when you are confronted with life situations. The pastors and ministers may not always be around to pray for you or lay hands on you in your time of need. Let the Holy Spirit suggest to you which word you need at each particular time of your need or the rhema word.

The Word of God is still with us today as we read the Scriptures, and it still has power to save, heal, and deliver from oppression. In it lies our provisions, healings, rest, finances, protection, and all-round provisions.

"The word of God is quick and powerful and sharper than any twoedged sword piercing even to the dividing asunder of soul and spirit and of the joints and marrow and is a discerner of the thoughts and intents of the heart" (Heb 4:12).

In as much as you have chosen the Christian faith and believed in Jesus Christ, the Word of God is indispensable. The spirit of God will use it to direct your path every now and then as you proceed in life. But if you choose to only go to church for fellowships and meetings and put your Bible back on the shelf, when you come back, it is not a good decision. When you encounter troubles in your way, apart from taking physical measures, you also need to face those situations with a positive attitude as you lean on God's promises for you. Learn to speak to yourself things like:

No weapon formed against me shall prosper.

I am the head and not the tail.

He sets the lonely in families.

There shall be no loss.

With long life, he shall satisfy me and show me his salvation.

Have an idea of what is being promised even though you may not be able to quote the whole Scripture word for word at the moment. And there are lots of promises in the Word.

Do not face your life struggles without the Word of God. Let the Word walk you through your life storms safely into the victorious side. Place your demands on the provisions in the Word of God or the promises of God.

Speak the word of God to yourself, and let yourself be encouraged. Cover yourself with the word by speaking the word over yourself and your situations. With your confessions, declare your belief and your faith.

A man of God once said the only reason his marriage did not break up few months after he got married to his wife was that he started engaging the Word of God. Speaking and encouraging himself with the Word of God and confessing positive words and God's promises over his wife and his marriage and in a matter of time things turned around for good and their marriage became wonderful.

Let God's Word be your maintenance tool. Allow God to maintain certain areas of your life as you speak God's word in agreement with the promises over your life.

Learn to make yourself live on the word of God so that your joy may be complete. It may not be automatic but that is the only sure way. It is not magic. Put God's word to work in your life, and let it yield its fruit for you.

Our shallowness in the knowledge of what the Word of God says, concerning our situations, put us in a state where we may not know what to do as regards the counsel of God.

What you are struggling to get in life, they are all hidden in the Word of God. Familiarize yourself with the words of God and promises of God. Let God hide the seeds of his Word in you that addresses various issues of life so that you can pull them up in times of need in the future, and war with them, so you can claim your victory over the enemy.

When we speak God's words, we are reaffirming God's thoughts, and we are saying that we believe in his promises for our lives.

As we repeat God's words, we give him materials to use to build up our lives. When we speak his Word, we allow God to fight our battles. We welcome him to be our defense. He uses the power and the anointing of his words to break the strongholds.

When we pray, we ask God to bring to pass in our lives the promise in his Word. We ask him to cause that particular verse in the Bible to work out or come alive in our lives.

So when you do not have any word or verse of Scripture in your hands, you are not cooperating with the Holy Spirit to fight for you. Instead, you are helping the enemy and the devil who will capitalize on the fact that you do not know what God has in store for you, making you to continue to live in fear all the time. "My people are destroyed for lack of knowledge" (Hos 4:6).

So you can only apply the Word of God that you know and understand. Things will change as God opens our eyes of revelation. The Word of God is for everybody.

Be encouraged to fight for your faith and blessings.

Don't be afraid to remind yourself of the fact that God is with you and will help you to defeat your enemy in the battle field, as it is written in the verse.

> God is our refuge and strength a very present help in trouble. Therefore, will not we fear though the earth be removed and though the mountains be covered into the midst of the sea Though the waters thereof roar and be troubled though the mountains shake with the welling thereof Salem. (Ps 46:13 KJV)

Say what the Word of God says about you and your situation, so you could have a turnaround. The Word of God is your land of Canaan. It is your promised land. So much blessings and future are embedded in the Word, waiting for you to harvest them as you give a voice to God's word.

The abundant life promised to us by Christ Jesus is hidden in his Word. If we acquaint ourselves with his Word, we are able to declare what God says over our lives so that we can be what his Word says we can become. We can also have what his Word declares we can have, and so that we can be able to do what his Word says we could do according to his grace and power.

As we do that, we see ourselves in the mirror of God's word, and we are able to reject what is not consistent with God's Words in our lives.

Let's be encouraged to speak to the storms and waves that we come across. Let us be able to say, "Peace, be still" like Jesus said to the waves while he was in the boat.

We can also come to a point in our lives where we can say to our mountains to move or to ask them to become a plain as we declare the Word of God to them by the grace of God, facing every struggle with God's word.

CONCLUSION

Salvation comes by hearing the message of salvation, receiving it in our hearts, and declaring or confessing our belief in the atonement of Christ Jesus for our inadequacies, sins, mistakes, and shortcomings with our mouths.

When we proclaim our faith, we are empowered to face our confrontations, and we receive power from God to overcome. We receive power to come out of the storms and turbulence of life. We receive power to stand on the top of our mountains or to tread upon our snakes and scorpions of life.

But what saith it. The word is nigh thee even in thy

mouth and in thy heart: that is the word of faith which we preach; That if thou shall confess with thy mouth the Lord Jesus and shall believe in thy heart that God hath raised him from the dead thou shall be saved. (Rom 10:8-17 KJV)

We profess our faith with our confession. We are able to say, "Peace, be still" to the storms, and we are able to move the mountains as we declare the word.

REFERENCES

Scriptural quotation in this book were taken from the King James Version, the New King James Version, and the New International Version bibles. Other references include the Webster's Dictionary.

AUTOBIOGRAPHY

This author is an alumni of the University of Ibadan, Ibadan, Nigeria. B.Ed., MLS

Contact email: martinaigwe8@gmail.com

ABOUT THE AUTHOR

Martina Ngozi Igwe read many books while she was growing up as a young girl. She came across books from great minds and wonderful authors. However, one more book she wished she would have read quite earlier in life is this book that she eventually wrote entitled Calm Your Storms and Move Your Mountains. A book replete with thoughtful inspirations.

www.ingramcontent.com/pod-product-compliance
Lightning Source LLC
Chambersburg PA
CBHW040800150426
42811CB00056B/1111